HOW
TO
BE
UN-
PROFESSIONAL
AT
WORK

Tips to Ensure Failure

MERRY BROWN

Additional books by Merry Brown

Non-fiction
The Food Addict: Recovering from Binge Eating Disorder &
Making Peace with Food

Fiction
The Four Families Series
Gold Manor Ghost House
Crimson Hall Ghost House
Silver Tree Ghost House
Serpent Star Ghost House (spring 2024)

The Exiled Trilogy
The Knowers
The Second Fall
The United

YA Books imprint
ISBN: 978-0-9899934-6-3
August 2023

All web links and addresses were valid at the time this book
was published. Due to the changing nature of the internet,
some links may no longer work.

Front and back cover designed by Merry Brown using Canva.

This book is dedicated to:

Dr. Christopher Brown, my best friend, ardent supporter, & husband.

INTRODUCTION: HOW TO USE THIS BOOK

"Everyone just needs to act professionally."

This sentiment is commonly expressed when people encounter an unmanaged work conflict.

Maintaining a professional reputation is vital for career advancement and fostering healthy work environments.

So... what does it mean to act professionally? What does it mean to you, your colleagues, and your organization?

This book is meant to serve as a starting point for conversation. If you don't know what to do, begin with what to avoid and move on from there. Get curious. Ask others. Build a team or organizational consensus.

Examining undesirable workplace behaviors can reveal how we should act. This book explores what it means to act unprofessionally as a way to think thoughtfully and productively about what professional behavior is, given differing roles and organizations.

Feel free to disagree with some of what you read here- I expect you will. The point of this book is to start a conversation, both within yourself and others, about what is and isn't professional behavior.

HOW TO BE UNPROFESSIONAL AT WORK TIPS

1. Be petty
2. Don't address work conflicts
3. Be late
4. Don't take responsibility for your actions
5. Try to get away with "it"
6. Be selfish
7. If someone disagrees with you, attack their character & competence
8. Disregard the needs & desires of others
9. Gossip
10. Don't keep your word
11. Think everyone is against you
12. Pit people against each other
13. Be lazy
14. Act as if the rules don't apply to you
15. Dress improperly
16. Hold grudges
17. Assume you know your coworker's opinions & ideas
18. Assume you know more than everyone else
19. Exaggerate
20. Boss colleagues around
21. Minimize the work of others
22. Overshare personal information with colleagues & clients
23. Don't proofread
24. Don't return calls (phones calls? Yuck.)
25. Don't return emails (in a timely manner)
26. Join a work faction

27. Listen to music loudly
28. Set the office temperature for your comfort
29. Let it mold
30. Don't ask questions
31. "Stay in your lane"
32. Ignore customers and clients
33. Yell
34. Brag
35. Mumble
36. Talk over your colleagues
37. Be late to meetings
38. Don't make (or read) the agenda
39. Don't read your work emails
40. Shame people for their political/religious beliefs
41. Talk until you run out of breath
42. Make it all about you
43. Steal your colleague's food
44. Don't clean your clothes
45. Take the last – and don't replace- roll of toilet paper
46. Assume it's someone else's job to clean up after you
47. Be clingy
48. Make jokes at other people's expense
49. Share a coworker's private information without their consent
50. Surprise your boss
51. Don't communicate with your boss
52. Don't communicate with your colleagues
53. Sabotage your colleagues
54. Spill company issues on your social media

55. Have a bad attitude
56. Be unpredictable
57. Expect others to tiptoe around your shifting mood
58. Humiliate others for their mistakes
59. Hold excessive meetings
60. Hold no meetings
61. Don't ask for help when you need it
62. Lie
63. Leave projects unfinished
64. Don't care about the quality of your work
65. Be done with learning
66. Work 24/7
67. Go to work sick
68. Don't take vacation
69. Assume work cannot function without you
70. Gatekeep data
71. Don't be transparent
72. Be unapproachable
73. Assume negative intent from others
74. Roll your eyes
75. Be stinky
76. Don't welcome questions
77. Ridicule others
78. Expect all to think like you
79. Complain
80. Set impossibly high standards

HOW TO BE **UN**-PROFESSIONAL AT WORK TIPS

How to be *Unprofessional* at work, tip #1:

BE
PETTY

How concerned are you with the trivial behaviors of your colleagues?

Do you magnify minor issues, hold grudges, or seek revenge over perceived slights and offenses?

Petty actions and attitudes create unnecessary conflict, tension, and drama at work, thereby damaging trust, respect, and goodwill.

Instead, embrace the sayings:

"Live and let live" & "Major on the majors"

Being overly concerned with what your colleagues are (and aren't) up to is a sign of small-mindedness and a desire to control the other adults around you.

You may wonder, "How do I know if I'm being petty or if my concerns about my colleague are legitimate?"

If you are genuinely asking this question, you're headed in the right direction. The next step is to talk to a trusted mentor, and one who won't simply tell you what is easy to hear.

From there, spend time reflecting as to what is and isn't your business at work.

Good luck!

Gaining a reputation for being petty will negatively impact your reputation as a professional.

DON'T ADDRESS WORK CONFLICTS

Why should I talk to my coworkers (or boss) about what's going on? They know what they're doing, and they clearly don't care about me or anyone else!

There are many reasons why people don't speak up at work when there's an issue, such as:
- fear of retaliation and making things worse
- fear of losing a job
- fear of conflict in general
- despair that anything will improve the situation

When you don't speak up, things won't change. The personal price of not dealing with workplace conflict is staggering.

Ultimately, learning to deal with conflict at work is about personal empowerment. You don't have to wait for others to solve your issues. You can!

Instead of hiding, act courageously and be an asset in your organization. Deal with workplace conflicts early, swiftly, and justly. If you develop basic conflict resolution skills and use them regularly, people will want you on their team.

Conflict is normal and expected at work. Let's deal with it.

Gaining a reputation for not addressing workplace conflicts will negatively impact your reputation as a professional.

How to be *Unprofessional* at work, tip #3:

BE
LATE

It's okay if I'm late (again), I know what I'm doing. And they don't need me right away.

It is interesting how many people feel getting to work late is no big deal. While it may be "no big deal" to you, it probably is to those around you.

So, what does it mean to be on time?

This differs widely for a whole host of reasons.

For some, the "rule" says be in at 9 a.m., but this is just a loose suggestion. The culture of this organization has it that as long as you are at your desk by 9:30 a.m., having gotten your morning drink and office chats in, you are on time.

For others, the "rule" states work begins at 8 a.m. However, the unwritten expectation is that you arrive by 7:45 a.m. at the latest so you can be ready to get to work when the shift changes at 8 a.m.

So, what does it mean to be on time where you work?

If you don't know the answer, ask your colleagues and boss. If you get this wrong, it will be to your detriment.

Gaining a reputation for being late can negatively impact your reputation as a professional.

DON'T TAKE RESPON- SIBILITY FOR YOUR ACTIONS

Why should I take responsibility for what happened? I mean, I just work here and it's not really my fault. She made me mad and he caused me to mess-up.

Yikes.

We've all worked with people who can't take their share of the blame when things go wrong. Do you want that person on your team? Probably not.

A giant red flag hangs over the person who thinks they never make mistakes, since:

- We all make mistakes.
- We all have bad days.
- We have all, at some point, failed to do our best work.

What mistakes have you made at work?

If you can't answer this question, take it as a reminder to become more self-aware.

Gaining a reputation for not taking responsibility for your actions will negatively impact your reputation as a professional.

How to be *Unprofessional* at work, tip #5:

TRY
TO
GET
AWAY
WITH
"IT"

Take what you can get. Leave early when you can. Do as little work as possible.

This work attitude is like that of a scheming kid, seeing what he can do behind the back of the teacher.

This is not how grown people behave.

This smells of passive-aggressiveness.

This looks like cowardice.

If you have an issue or problem, address it. Don't sneak around.

Gaining a reputation for trying to get away with "it" will negatively impact your reputation as a professional.

BE
SELFISH

Why shouldn't you always get the newest office gadget, chair, computer, first crack at picking vacation dates, the best parking spot, what you want when it comes to resource allocation and direction of the department you're in.

Why shouldn't you always get your way?

You are an important part of your organization. Your thoughts, beliefs, needs, and desires matter... just as much as the thoughts, beliefs, needs, and desires of your colleagues.

Practice sharing and considering the needs of your colleagues. Being generous and considerate of those around you (ironically?) is the best path towards getting your needs met at work.

Gaining a reputation for being selfish will negatively impact your reputation as a professional.

IF SOMEONE DISAGREES WITH YOU, ATTACK THEIR CHARACTER & COMPETENCE

What should you do when someone disagrees with your ideas and proposals at work?

You can choose to verbally attack your colleague, degrading them in order to assert your will and dominance. I mean... you can do this, but at what cost?

Conflict is normal. We should expect - and welcome! - healthy conflict at work. Without friction, how are we going to bring diverse ideas to the table and harness the power of the team?

Name calling and degrading behavior towards colleagues shuts down the free exchange of ideas and innovation.

It is a sign of emotional immaturity to verbally attack colleagues. Anyone who acts in this uncivil way is not fit for management. This behavior should not be tolerated by anyone at work.

Gaining a reputation for attacking people who disagree with you will negatively impact your reputation as a professional.

How to be *Unprofessional* at work, tip #8:

DISREGARD THE NEEDS & DESIRES OF OTHERS

When you're at a meeting, do you listen to your colleagues? Do you care what they have to say or do you minimize their contributions?

First and foremost, we have an ethical responsibility to treat people with dignity and respect.

When we choose to ignore the needs and wishes of our colleagues, we wear away at their basic sense of belonging that is crucial for individuals and teams to function efficiently and achieve success.

This kind of behavior also violates the golden rule: treat others the way you want to be treated. This basic principle is fundamental to promote positive human interactions.

Gaining a reputation for disregarding the needs and desires of your colleagues will negatively impact your reputation as a professional.

How to be *Unprofessional* at work, tip #9:

GOSSIP

Gossip is fun! I love to talk about others. And besides, it's totally normal. Everyone does it.

An action can be done by many, but it doesn't make it right. Something can be "normal" and unethical.

- Gossip contains accusations and assumptions about another person's intention.
- Gossip focuses on the past.
- Gossip does not look for constructive solutions.
- Gossip is essentially a cowardly, uncivil act that kicks people when they are down.
- Gossiping isn't the same as venting. Venting to a trusted colleague is about you, your perceptions, and how to move forward.

Rule of thumb: If you wouldn't say it to the person, don't say it about the person.

If you want to be trusted at work and strive to treat your colleagues well, refrain from gossiping.

Gaining a reputation for being a gossip will negatively impact your reputation as a professional.

How to be *Unprofessional* at work, tip #10:

DON'T KEEP YOUR WORD

You know those people at work who say one thing and do another?

You know those people at work who you don't trust will follow through on what they said they'd do?

Conversely, how do you feel about and act towards those in your organization you trust will do what they say?

Rule of thumb: Do what you say you are going to do.

Sometimes, we plan to do something, but due to unforeseen circumstances we no longer can. This certainly happens.

In this case, talk with your colleagues and/or supervisor and make a new plan.

Gaining a reputation for not keeping your word will negatively impact your reputation as a professional.

How to be *Unprofessional* at work, tip #11:

THINK EVERYONE IS AGAINST YOU

You know those people who have decided the world is against them? No one is to be trusted.

This mindset can be a self-fulfilling prophecy. Thinking "everyone is out to get me" breeds certain kinds of work behaviors, such as suspicion, an inability to listen and work well with others, catastrophizing, and selfishness.

This person has a chip on their shoulder, defeated before they begin.

It's not pleasant working with someone like this because you are battling their unseen demons, usually being asked to pacify them, lest you unintentionally reinforce their mantra that they are the victim.

If this is you, how is this serving you? What are you gaining? I'm telling you this is not winning you strong and fruitful work relationships because you are basically asking others to walk on eggshells around you.

(Is it *possible* everyone at work actually is working against you? Sure. I don't know you or your circumstances. But, if this happens everywhere you go, chances are it's you and not them.)

Gaining a reputation for thinking and acting as if everyone is against you will negatively impact your reputation as a professional.

How to be *Unprofessional* at work, tip #12:

PIT PEOPLE AGAINST EACH OTHER

Working both sides of the room to get your way? Getting people fighting so you can emerge the peacemaker or savior?

This strategy is short-sighted and will backfire. When you create chaos in your work environment, you invite distrust, resentment, decreased morale, stress, burnout, and lack of collaboration. Making factions at work blocks improvements, engagement, high productivity, and a respectful work environment.

You are not a contestant on a "reality" show. You are at work, trying to make a living to pay your bills... as are your coworkers.

Pitting people against each other is manipulative and selfish behavior.

Gaining a reputation for pitting people against each other will negatively impact your reputation as a professional.

How to be *Unprofessional* at work, tip #13:

BE
LAZY

There's an art to working the *right* amount. Aristotle calls this "The Golden Mean," finding the excellent path between the extremes of too much and too little.

Being lazy and unproductive can make it difficult for you to advance in your career. Employers are looking for employees who are driven, productive, and add value to the organization. If you are consistently failing to meet expectations, you may not be considered for promotions or other opportunities.

It's possible your current work violates The Golden Mean. It is important to clearly understand the expectations at work so you can decide if this is an organization that has reasonable work requirements.

If you're not sure what counts as lazy and unproductive behavior where you work, ask.

Gaining a reputation for being lazy and unproductive will negatively impact your reputation as a professional.

ACT AS IF THE RULES DON'T APPLY TO YOU

Everyone else needs to be on time, but you don't.

Everyone else needs to submit their work by the deadline, but not you.

Everyone else needs to follow proper procedures and protocols, but you're exempt.

This sounds ridiculous, right? Yet, most of us have known colleagues to behave this way (and, quite possibly, we've acted/thought this way on occasion).

When employees believe that some people are excused from following the rules, it creates a sense of unfairness and resentment. If you consistently break/bend the rules to suit your own needs, you may be seen as someone who is untrustworthy or difficult to work with.

Gaining a reputation for acting as if the rules don't apply to you will negatively impact your reputation as a professional.

How to be *Unprofessional* at work, tip #15:

DRESS IMPROPERLY

There is a reason dress codes differ from place to place. What is appropriate and professional for the lifeguard differs from the surgeon.

Know the dress expectations of your profession and organization. Get specifics.

What if the standards are unreasonable or outdated?

Bring this issue to the attention of your organization with data as to why it is out of date (new industry standards, societal shift, etc.) and make a case for change.

Gaining a reputation for dressing unprofessionally will negatively impact your reputation as a professional.

How to be *Unprofessional* at work, tip #16:

HOLD GRUDGES

Holding grudges can lead to a lack of trust between coworkers, which makes it hard to build strong working relationships, delegate tasks, share information, and communicate effectively.

If you are known as someone who holds grudges, people will be wary of working with you, lest they get on your "bad side." This is a form of emotional manipulation.

It's important to address conflicts and issues with colleagues in a professional and respectful manner, rather than holding onto negative feelings and resentment. By resolving conflicts and working collaboratively with others, a more positive and productive work environment is created for everyone involved.

What if someone holds a grudge against you? First, you are not responsible for other people's thoughts. I encourage you to take responsibility for any mistakes you've made and make amends. Beyond that, treat your coworker with dignity and respect.

We can't command people to "let it go" on our timetable.

Gaining a reputation for holding grudges will negatively impact your reputation as a professional.

ASSUME YOU KNOW YOUR COWORKER'S OPINIONS & IDEAS

No need to consult your colleague, you've heard it all before. You know what they think. Right?

I've felt insulted, misunderstood, and minimized when colleagues assume they know what I think without asking. What about you?

Assuming you know your colleague's opinions and ideas can lead to misunderstandings and disrespect, limit the potential for new ideas, and damage working relationships.

You don't know what's going on in your colleague's mind.

It's important to approach colleagues with an open mind, listen to their perspectives, and respect their individuality.

Decide to hang up your hat as the office mind reader.

Gaining a reputation for assuming you know your colleague's opinions & ideas without first talking to them will negatively impact your reputation as a professional.

ASSUME YOU KNOW MORE THAN EVERYONE ELSE

Are you the smartest one in the room?

Do you, objectively, know more than everyone else?

You undoubtedly know more about some things than your colleagues... but everything? I can confidently say this is a false belief.

YOU ARE smart and capable. Assuming that you know more than everyone else at work, however, can lead to a negative work environment, hinder collaboration and productivity, and limit personal and professional growth.

It's important to approach work with a humble and open mindset, acknowledging the knowledge and expertise of others in order to create a positive and dynamic work environment.

Behaving as though you know more than everyone else often reflects poorly on your self-awareness and emotional maturity.

Gaining a reputation for being a know-it-all will negatively impact your reputation as a professional.

How to be *Unprofessional* at work, tip #19:

EXAGGERATE

This is the best idea ever, no need for discussion!

I've given this presentation a million times!

Colleagues who exaggerate are the worst!

When someone exaggerates, they are presenting information that is not entirely accurate or truthful, which can lead others to doubt their reliability and honesty. This can make it difficult to build strong working relationships and lead to breakdowns in communication and collaboration.

It's important to be truthful and accurate in your communications at work, even if it means acknowledging limitations or areas where you may need additional support. By being honest and transparent, you can build trust and credibility with your colleagues.

Gaining a reputation for exaggerating will negatively impact your reputation as a professional.

BOSS COLLEAGUES AROUND

Have you ever felt your colleagues were clueless and lucky to have you around to tell them what to do?

Sometimes our colleagues **are** at a loss and better off for having us on their team. But bossing them around? Directing the work of peers is bad form.

Do you like being bossed around? Even if you're the boss, "bossing people around" is unlikely to achieve the long-term results you desire: independence, innovation, belonging, growth, high performance, etc.

Bossing people, even if you're the boss (!), treats grown adults as children. Your employees/colleagues are not kids. Treat them like adults.

Rule of thumb: Don't boss people around.

Gaining a reputation for bossing colleagues around will negatively impact your reputation as a professional.

MINIMIZE THE WORK OF OTHERS

Why not take all the credit? You're the most important team member, right?

This way of thinking offers a false sense of self and often results in resentment, lack of innovation, and decreased trust.

Why do people minizine the contributions of others?

- Sometimes people are not aware or are not paying attention to who is doing what.
- Sometimes it's because people feel threatened by the accomplishments of others.
- Sometimes people want to harm their colleagues.

When you specifically recognize and value the contributions of team members, you are laying the cultural foundation for collaboration, innovation, and respect.

When you recognize and value the contributions of others, your social capital at work increases because you are seen as a reasonable, caring, and just person.

Gaining a reputation for minimizing the contributions of others will negatively impact your reputation as a professional.

OVERSHARE PERSONAL INFORMATION WITH COLLEAGUES & CLIENTS

- All of my thoughts, all of the time
- The details of my doctor visits
- A lengthy, step-by-step explanation of my latest hobby

It can be difficult to figure out what is acceptable to share at the office and what is best left unsaid. Therefore, it's worth spending time thinking about what personal information is and isn't acceptable to share at work.

Before you decide to share personal information at work, ask yourself:

- Given where I work, why is it acceptable to share this private information here?
- Is this conversation about my private life going to make my colleague/client uncomfortable?
- Is work the appropriate place to share this information? If so, why?
- Is this conversation building bridges or putting up barriers?
- Am I okay with the content of this conversation being overheard by others?
- Why am I sharing this information?

Gaining a reputation for oversharing personal information with colleagues & clients will negatively impact your reputation as a professional.

How to be *Unprofessional* at work, tip #23:

DON'T PROOF- READ

You got it done! Yay! Now send it.

The question is, is it really done? Have you reviewed and re-read that email, that proposal, that newsletter, that business text, that piece of copy properly?

Typos happen. But they are mistakes.

Be proactive. Read and re-read. Have several sets of eyes review your work. Send it through an AI generator, looking for mistakes.

This may sound like a lot of work, but once you've established a system and pattern for how you will review your written work, it becomes second nature.

If your written communication is continually riddled with problems, an unintended message may be sent to your colleagues such as:

You don't care about details,
or
You're OK with mistakes,
or
You don't even see the sloppiness of your work.

Professionals pay attention to details. Like it or not, that's the way it is.

Gaining a reputation for doing sloppy work will negatively impact your reputation as a professional.

DON'T RETURN CALLS

Phones calls? Yuck.

Return calls? What is this, 1985??? No one cares about calls anymore, right?

Wrong.

From phone calls to texts, emails to Google Docs, in person to online meetings, there are lots of forms of communication to choose from. And people have different preferences.

Communicating effectively at work requires flexibility. Work is not only about how YOU *like* to communicate.

Rule of thumb: When a colleague or client reaches out to you, return their communication using the form of communication in which they sent it.

If your organization doesn't routinely use a certain form of communication, let the person know and discuss how to move forward with a form of communication that works for you both.

Gaining a reputation for not returning calls will negatively impact your reputation as a professional.

How to be *Unprofessional* at work, tip #25:

DON'T RETURN EMAILS

in a timely manner

I'll get to it when I get to it. They can just wait for me. I'm in no hurry. It doesn't really matter if it takes weeks or months to return those emails.

It's entirely true that professionals don't run around constantly putting out fires, at the beck and call of whoever's demanding their attention.

However, if you are trying to build a professional reputation as a trusted and competent employee, people need to know and trust that when they reach out to you, you will get back in touch with them in a reasonable and timely manner.

Gaining a reputation for not returning communication in a timely manner will negatively impact your reputation as a professional.

How to be *Unprofessional* at work, tip #26:

JOIN A WORK FACTION

It's us versus them. I need to pick a side.

Woah. Hold on there.

If there really are factions where you work... this is a serious red flag that needs to be addressed. Not addressing work factions will be to everybody's detriment, including the organization's.

A professional is seen as fair, thoughtful, and reliable, which is the opposite of game playing and this kind of petty office politics.

Resist getting drawn into office battles and choosing sides.

Gaining a reputation for choosing sides will negatively impact your reputation as a professional.

LISTEN TO MUSIC LOUDLY

It's your office.

It's your workspace.

Why shouldn't you listen to what you want, when you want, and at the volume you want?

When you're in a shared space, professionals are mindful of others. Professionals don't think the office, warehouse, or store is only a place for them to enjoy.

Even if you don't care about being a professional, decide to treat people with civility at work.

Gaining a reputation for listening to music too loudly will negatively impact your reputation as a professional.

SET
THE
TEMPERATURE
FOR
YOUR
COMFORT

Too hot? Too cold? No one else really cares about the office temperature, not like you. Why should you be concerned if your colleagues are freezing or sweating? They are welcome to put on a sweater or get a fan.

The temperature settings at work bring a lot of opinions and feelings. To disregard the desires of your colleagues and only focus on what you want is a sign of unrealistic self-importance.

What is the temperature set at where you work? Why? Who gets to decide? Why them?

Gaining a reputation for disregarding colleagues' temperature concerns will negatively impact your reputation as a professional.

LET
IT
MOLD

You brought your lunch to work, but you didn't get around to eating it.

You put your lunch leftovers in the shared work fridge and forgot it. And now it sits there, for weeks. No need to clean it out because somebody always throws that stuff away.

Some people really care about the state of the communal fridge. Others don't.

Don't be lulled into the sense that you aren't responsible for what you put in the fridge because you personally don't care about a messy fridge. This is a shared workspace and not your personal home environment.

Rule of thumb: Clean up after yourself.

Gaining a reputation for not cleaning up your refrigerator mess will negatively impact your reputation as a professional.

DON'T
ASK
QUESTIONS

Not sure what you're supposed to do? Your boss unclear?

Don't know how to run that program, work that piece of machinery, make that presentation?

Many people are afraid or hesitant to ask questions because they feel this makes them look incompetent.

Questions are normal. Questions are a sign you're engaged and want to do excellent work.

Time permitting, avoid asking questions until you've reasonably investigated (e.g., Google search, etc.). If you still have questions, ask.

Ask informed questions. Say to your boss/colleague, "I looked here and there. I found this and that." Then ask questions for clarity.

Gaining a reputation for not asking questions for clarity when needed will negatively impact your reputation as a professional.

"STAY IN YOUR LANE..."

...exclusively

Wait. What? I thought I was supposed to "stay in my lane." I do my job and you do yours, right?

Yes and no.

If you're on a team and you specialize in one area, and your teammates in theirs, this recommendation is not about being interfering, but curious. The more you understand how your work fits into the work of your team and broader division/organization, the better your contributions will be.

It is also a sign of professionalism to continually grow and develop. Stay in your lane when appropriate, while also being agile, flexible, and interested in learning.

Gaining a reputation for not being willing to look outside of your narrow field of work will negatively impact your reputation as a professional.

How to be *Unprofessional* at work, tip #32:

IGNORE CUSTOMERS & CLIENTS

So annoying, aren't they?

They walk into work and want to be served.
They call and want your attention.
They email and expect a response.

What – do they think the world revolves around them?

This is the attitude, either overtly or unintentionally, some workers give off. And it shows. And we feel it when we walk into that restaurant or interact with that businessperson.

If you ignore customers and/or treat them as a burden, expect to lose credibility and possibly your job.

Gaining a reputation for ignoring clients will negatively impact your reputation as a professional.

How to be *Unprofessional* at work, tip #33:

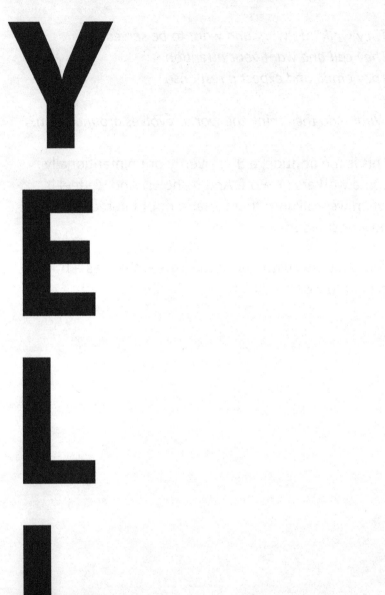

These people don't understand unless you raise your voice! **NO**

These people are responsible for making me mad! **NO**

These people deserve to be yelled at! **NO**

Yelling, in this context, is not about raising your voice to be heard over loud work music or heavy machinery. The kind of yelling I'm talking about is used to control, berate, belittle, and/or embarrass colleagues.

You are at work. The rules of basic civility apply, which means **NO** yelling.

Gaining a reputation for yelling at colleagues will negatively impact your reputation as a professional.

How to be *Unprofessional* at work, tip #34:

BRAG

First off, you are probably a great human being. You probably have accomplished loads in your life.

YAY!

Humans are (can be) awesome! Look at all your awesome successes!!!

So... why *not* brag?

At work, when you brag, you broadcast to colleagues that "it" is all about and because of YOU.

The bragger says, "LOOK AT ALL THE THINGS I'VE DONE. ME. I DID THESE THINGS BY MYSELF!"

Herein lies the rub. No, you didn't. No one is an island. This is taking credit for what is not true.

Instead, go for what Aristotle calls "Proper Pride." This is looking squarely at who you are and your accomplishments, while not over – or under – assessing them.

Gaining a reputation for bragging will negatively impact your reputation as a professional.

How to be *Unprofessional* at work, tip #35:

MUMBLE

What was that again? What did you say?

At work, can people understand what you are saying?

Mumbling may signify to others a lack of confidence.

Consider how to successfully communicate with your colleagues. Are any hearing impaired? Do you have colleagues working in an environment that is not in their native language?

Speak clearly and confidently to the best of your ability to effectively communicate with those around you.

Note: What it means to speak "clearly and confidently" will differ depending on the culture and context you find yourself in.

Gaining a reputation for mumbling will negatively impact your reputation as a professional.

TALK OVER YOUR COLLEAGUES

Who cares what they have to say? You have something more important, more timely, more relevant, and frankly, more interesting to say, right?

Even if the above is true to a certain degree, it doesn't change the fact that talking over someone is rude and unprofessional.

A sure sign you aren't a team player is the tendency to ignore and dismiss your coworkers by talking over them at meetings.

Allow others to finish their thoughts before contributing.

Gaining a reputation for talking over your colleagues when they are talking will negatively impact your reputation as a professional.

How to be *Unprofessional* at work, tip #37:

BE LATE TO MEETINGS

Your Zoom meeting starts at 9am and you're not there.

Your in-person meeting was scheduled to begin at 10am, and you're nowhere to be found.

Who cares? Everyone there – to some extent. When you show up late to meetings, you are telling everyone you:

A. Are unprepared
B. Don't care
C. Both A & B

Respect yourself and others by being on time to meetings.

What if everyone is habitually late to meetings? Hold an open exchange and talk about it. Decide what "on time" is and what happens when people don't value the time and schedule of others.

Gaining a reputation for being late to meetings will negatively impact your reputation as a professional.

DON'T
MAKE
(OR READ)
THE
AGENDA

They are lucky you scheduled or showed up to their stupid meeting. I mean, who meets anymore? Aren't meetings dead?? Shouldn't this all just be an email???

Your philosophical issues with meetings are irrelevant when you've either scheduled or been asked to attend a mandatory meeting.

If you are in charge, **ALWAYS** have an agenda. Even for a "quick" meeting.

If you are attending, **ALWAYS** read through the agenda and prepare accordingly.

Gaining a reputation for not making and/or not reading meeting agendas will negatively impact your reputation as a professional.

DON'T READ YOUR WORK EMAILS

Another email from your boss?
Another email from HR?
Another email from that colleague?
Another email from that professional association you're a member of?

Too many emails! And who cares? I mean, who puts important information in an email? If it's really important, "they'll" tell me at a meeting or when they see me in the hall, right?

Nope.

Whether or not you like email (or whatever messaging software your organization uses) is irrelevant. It's your responsibility to read work emails. Read the *entire* email AND respond when appropriate. This is basic work etiquette.

Stay informed and responsive at work.

Gaining a reputation for not reading your work emails will negatively impact your reputation as a professional.

How to be *Unprofessional* at work, tip #40:

SHAME PEOPLE FOR THEIR POLITICAL/ RELIGIOUS BELIEFS

Can you even believe she thinks that? That's crazy!
Can you even believe he voted that way? What a selfish,
self-important ignorant loser!

I can't believe any rational person would hold that social
view. They really believe the government has the right to
do that?

Hey – you. Why do you think everyone needs to believe what you do and see the world the way you see it? Are you the only person who is smart and has thought things through? Are you the only one who has good reasons for your beliefs?

And, for arguments sake, let's suppose your coworker does hold extreme views on religion or politics. You're at work – not a bar (unless you work at a bar). This is not the time or place to try to make people feel bad for their beliefs or shame them into coming over to your side.

And, besides, ever heard the expression, "Live and let live?" Do you believe diversity is a good? Then act like it.

THIS IS WORK. So... WORK. Do not make a habit of being the judge of who is "good" or "bad" at work based on their personal beliefs. Instead, focus on getting work done and treating colleagues with civility (at a minimum).

Gaining a reputation for shaming people because of their political or religious beliefs will negatively impact your reputation as a professional.

How to be *Unprofessional* at work, tip #41:

TALK UNTIL YOU RUN OUT OF BREATH

You have a lot to say. Great!

You have tons of ideas. Wonderful!

You like chatting with your colleagues and clients. Fabulous!

There is a vast difference between liking to talk with those around you and treating them like a brick wall.

No one wants to be talked-at. You know that feeling you get when someone drones on and on, and if you substituted a cardboard cutout of yourself that periodically says, "Uh huh," they wouldn't know the difference?

Do people say "they can't get a word in edgewise" around you?

Don't be that person. Real conversations involve give and take. In real conversations, we treat the other person with respect by valuing and wanting to hear from them.

Gaining a reputation for talking at people and not listening will negatively impact your reputation as a professional.

How to be *Unprofessional* at work, tip #42:

MAKE IT ALL ABOUT YOU

There's this scene in a movie where a vain stage actor is explaining why she's late to rehearsal. In the middle of her pedicure, her pedicurist had a heart attack and plunged a stick into her toe. It was just awful for her.

Yes, her toe experienced mild discomfort. Yes, she was then late to practice. But... what about the pedicurist?

You are important. What's going on at work has an effect on you. But not only you.

The world doesn't revolve around you.

If you act as if everything – wins, losses, inconveniences – is about you, you are not only wrong, you send the message to your colleagues that you find them unimportant and disposable.

If this is the message your colleagues receive from you, working in a fruitful, collaborative, and productive way will likely not happen.

Gaining a reputation for making everything about you will negatively impact your reputation as a professional.

STEAL YOUR COLLEAGUE'S FOOD

Ever bring your lunch to work and have somebody else eat it?

Anybody ever take your leftovers?

Anyone ever eat the granola bars or treats you brought for yourself at work?

Don't. Eat. Other. People's. Food. Without. Asking.

People are funny about food. We have preferences. We get excited. We plan. We act like Pavlov's dogs, thinking about the food we're going to eat next. Or at least some of us do.

So, the next time you are tempted to rifle through the fridge at work, just remember, a sure way to make enemies at work is to take food that doesn't belong to you.

Don't be that person.

Gaining a reputation for taking your colleague's food will negatively impact your reputation as a professional.

How to be *Unprofessional* at work, tip #44:

DON'T CLEAN YOUR CLOTHES

They are lucky you showed up for work - and with clothes on! (I mean, for a year-and-a-half or more you may have worn pajamas to work during the pandemic at your makeshift home office.)

Yes, you need to dress professionally. And what it means to dress professionally is dependent on your profession and your work environment.

- Do you arrive at work covered in dirt?
- Do you arrive at work covered in pet hair?
- Do you arrive at work covered in foodstuffs?
- Do you arrive at work wearing stinky clothes?

Whatever your work environment, your clothes need to be clean. What counts as unclean clothes, you ask?

What it means for clothes to be clean may vary due to a lot of circumstances. If you don't know, ask. Always ask.

Rule of thumb: Arrive at work with clean, relatively freshly laundered clothes, that smell culturally acceptable.

Gaining a reputation for wearing dirty clothes to work will negatively impact your reputation as a professional.

How to be *Unprofessional* at work, tip #45:

TAKE THE LAST

– AND DON'T REPLACE-

ROLL OF TOILET PAPER

Do I really need to include this?

For obvious reasons, if you take the last roll, you need to replace it. Or, at the very least, alert the person who replenishes the rolls to the current bathroom situation.

Why should you do this? It's not your job, right?

WRONG.

It's your job to be minimally decent at work and to care about others, not just yourself. If you cannot be bothered to think about the next person who enters that room and finds themselves without a square to assist them... I mean, yikes. That's what it means to be selfish at work.

Part of being a professional is the recognition that others are important too. The organization is not all about you, even if you're the CEO.

Gaining a reputation for not restocking the toilet paper will negatively impact your reputation as a professional.

ASSUME IT'S SOMEONE ELSE'S JOB TO CLEAN UP AFTER YOU

Kate loves coffee. She loves to drink out of a ceramic mug and doesn't like the way a lid feels, so she doesn't use one. Why is this a problem? She's known for dribbling coffee down the hall, here and there, and on occasion, not cleaning it up.

After all, it's not your job to clean at work. You don't take out your trash, vacuum the rugs, sweep everything up, mop, dust, etc. (unless that is your actual job). And since it's not your job to clean up, why clean up after your messes?

There's a big difference between doing the routine cleaning of an office space and cleaning up your little scraps of paper at the copier hole punch, or washing out your mug and putting it away, or wiping down the microwave after you heated up your lunch.

It is your job, as a human person, to clean up after yourself.

Gaining a reputation for not cleaning up after yourself will negatively impact your reputation as a professional.

How to be *Unprofessional* at work, tip #47:

BE
CLINGY

Being at work can feel tricky and scary and lonely. So why not choose a person and stick to them like glue?

Not only can it be annoying to your coworkers if you attach yourself to them, but it can limit you at your job.

You may be treating your coworkers as a kind of security blanket, so that you don't *feel* you need to branch out and make connections, network, and learn for yourself.

It's good to have mentors. And how great is it when a mentor is a coworker! Ask them questions. Take notice of how they present themselves at work. Communicate regularly and seek advice when needed.

However, at work you need to stand on your own (to a great extent).

Gaining a reputation for being clingy will negatively impact your reputation as a professional.

MAKE JOKES AT OTHER PEOPLE'S EXPENSE

Funny one, the way you took down your coworker by making fun of their: height, weight, protected status, identity, age, income, background, mistake.

Nope. Not work appropriate.

Hey, I'm not the joke police. I'm not going to tell you that joke didn't get a laugh. And with a joke, as with most things, intentions matter, but what also matters (more) is how the person felt being subjected to that joke.

Lots of times we "joke" in a passive-aggressive way. And most know it wasn't "just a joke."

I know these are tricky times. The rules of society are changing as to what is/isn't a work appropriate joke, so I'm giving you TWO rules of thumb:

Rule of thumb #1: If you think (at all) you shouldn't say it/joke about it, then DON'T.

Rule of thumb #2: If the joke is at the expense of the other (AKA they may feel targeted or embarrassed), DON'T say it. Not even to your work friends.

Gaining a reputation for making jokes at other people's expense will negatively impact your reputation as a professional.

SHARE COWORKER'S PRIVATE INFO WITHOUT THEIR CONSENT

OH.MY.WORD. You will never believe what I heard about Claude!!! Did you know he was recently diagnosed with ADHD? Can you believe it?

Unless Claude told you that you can share his new diagnosis with the office, don't do it. That is his information to share, if he chooses.

It's not that you can't share private information, ever. Imagine a scenario where Claude discovers he has cancer and must go in for immediate surgery. He's going to be out of the office for the next few months and Claude has asked you to share this information, because it's too painful for him to have to tell everybody.

The issue here is malicious gossip. Refrain from telling the business of others unless you have been given express and clear permission to do so. And even then, talking about a sensitive topic involving another takes a certain level of respect and dignity.

Gaining a reputation for sharing a coworker's private information without their consent will negatively impact your reputation as a professional.

How to be *Unprofessional* at work, tip #50:

SURPRISE YOUR BOSS

by withholding bad news

Angry client?
Customer got injured in the store?
Ran out of product?
Getting a bad review in the newspaper?
Forgot to book the event space for the conference 1,000 people have already RSVPed for?

No need to tell the boss, they'll find out soon enough. Besides, what can you do about it now? You're already in trouble.

Well, you may be in trouble, but there is something you can do about it. Tell your boss.

Bosses are **FAMOUS** for not liking bad surprises.

When mistakes are made, which will happen, professionals admit the problem as soon as they become aware of it and tell whomever they report to. The sooner the better to minimize the harm.

If you don't let your boss know the bad things going on, they will lose trust in you.

Gaining a reputation for withholding bad news from your boss will negatively impact your reputation as a professional.

DON'T COMMUNICATE WITH YOUR BOSS

You know what you're up to, why tell your boss?

You know the progress of the projects you're working on, why tell your boss?

You know where you are, then why tell your boss?

You know why you're late, so why tell your boss?

You're a grown professional, therefore, why do you need to tell your boss anything?

I get it. But there's a wide scale (like the Grand Canyon) between telling your boss everything and telling your boss nothing.

Your boss needs to know what you're up to. Even if it's the case your boss doesn't really care, for your own professional protection, tell your boss.

Find the balance between over and under communicating with your boss. Let your boss know, in the right way, what you're up to, what your plans are, what your progress is, if you need any assistance, and other relevant information. Make this a habit.

This means you need to learn how your boss wants to be communicated with.

Gaining a reputation for not communicating with your boss will negatively impact your reputation as a professional.

DON'T COMMUNICATE WITH YOUR COLLEAGUES

They are your colleagues, not your boss. You owe them nothing. Right?

You don't report to them, and they have no business being in your business.

It's true you don't report to them, and they certainly have no business being in your personal business. But work business that directly and relevantly affects them? That's different.

Keep your colleagues informed, consistently, on relevant work information they need to know to:

1. Get their work done
2. Contribute to a healthy work environment

Gaining a reputation for not consistently communicating with your colleagues will negatively impact your reputation as a professional.

How to be *Unprofessional* at work, tip #53:

SABOTAGE YOUR COWORKERS

Wide is the path to throwing your colleagues under the bus. There are lots of ways to make your coworkers' lives harder and damage their careers.

You can do this by not giving them their due credit, gossiping about them, starting rumors, not pulling your weight, being mean and unthoughtful, actively plotting to make them look like fools.

But why act this way? To what end? Revenge, "justice," personal glory?

Instead of actively plotting against colleagues, try to be better at your job. Instead of worrying about what others are or aren't doing, focus on your own work ethic and cultivate your own excellence.

If you choose, instead, to harm colleagues, look out. You will get what you dish out. **Karma knows where to find you.**

Gaining a reputation for sabotaging colleagues will negatively impact your reputation as a professional.

How to be *Unprofessional* at work, tip #54:

SPILL COMPANY ISSUES ON YOUR SOCIAL MEDIA

My work has NO RIGHT to tell me what to say or not say on my social media accounts. I will say/write whatever I want.

This is a naïve view of the world.

You might be able to post whatever you want, but that doesn't mean you are free from the consequences.

For example, let's say you have a fight with a family member. You go online and talk about how awful that person is. What do you think will happen next? What do you think the effect of that post might be a year from now? Five years from now?

Be careful and thoughtful before you burn a bridge.

If you post something on a public account that trashes people in your organization or the organization itself, don't be surprised when people get the impression that you are reckless, impulsive, selfish, self-serving, untrustworthy... shall I go on?

Gaining a reputation for dragging people you work with on social media will negatively impact your reputation as a professional.

HAVE
A
BAD
ATTITUDE

My attitude is my business. You can have my work. I'll answer the phones or do whatever this job calls for. But that's all you're paying for. You're paying for my work. You don't also get my attitude!

This is one approach to work. And most of us have worked with people who think and act this way. It certainly isn't pleasant to be around these attitude vampires.

What is a bad attitude? I suppose it boils down to the vibe you send out. When people approach you, do they worry you're going to yell at them or mistreat them in some way? Do people feel like they are bothering you simply for existing? Yeah, that's a sign of a bad attitude.

If you want to get ahead in business, you've got to pay attention to the vibe you send out. I'm not talking about always having a fake smile on your face, but how do people generally feel once they leave your presence?

If you don't know, ask (& don't just ask friends who won't give you an honest assessment).

Gaining a reputation for having a bad attitude will negatively impact your reputation as a professional.

How to be *Unprofessional* at work, tip #56:

BE UN- PREDICT -ABLE

Hey, anyone know if Bob's gonna be here today?

Anybody know if Sally got that project done on time?

I wonder if Kyle submitted our timesheets this week?

For two straight weeks, Anita remembered to order enough materials for the event. I wonder if she'll make it a 3-week streak?!?

I wonder if the boss will be in a good or a rotten mood today?

Unless you're a professional comedian or magician, being unpredictable at work is not a good look.

Be reliable and consistent. Be the kind of worker people can count on to be on time, prepared, and even tempered.

Gaining a reputation for being unpredictable will negatively impact your reputation as a professional.

EXPECT OTHERS TO TIPTOE AROUND YOUR SHIFTING MOOD

People need to respect you. They need to be sensitive to your moods. They need to "read" the signs and do their homework before they approach you.

Yes?

Well... yes to the above, but in a way where you act as an adult, and so do your coworkers. If people feel they are "walking on eggshells" around you, this means you are volatile, unpredictable, "moody," and probably unpleasant some of the time.

Knock. It. Off.

No one should "tiptoe" around you. You are not a child and work is not YOUR DOMAIN ALONE. There are other people who work there who matter just as much as you do.

You – AND NO ONE ELSE – are in charge of your mood. Unless you are clinically, medically, unstable, it is up to you to pull it together and not make it a miserable experience for others to have to work with you.

You do not need to be friends with your colleagues, but they shouldn't have to dance around you like you're a minefield.

If you want to progress at work, you've got to figure out a way to be consistently approachable at work.

Gaining a reputation for expecting others to walk on eggshells around you will negatively impact your reputation as a professional.

How to be *Unprofessional* at work, tip #58:

HUMILIATE OTHERS FOR THEIR MISTAKES

People will make mistakes.

You will make mistakes.

We will make large and small mistakes at work. This will happen.

Some mistakes are not really our fault, and some are.

Regardless of the reason behind the mistake, there is no room for scolding or shaming a coworker.

Consequences? Sure.

Humiliation? **NEVER.**

Since we know we and our coworkers will make mistakes that negatively affect us, decide now how you will address the mistakes while also treating the mistake-maker with dignity and basic human regard.

Gaining a reputation for humiliating coworkers for mistakes will negatively impact your reputation as a professional.

How to be *Unprofessional* at work, tip #59:

HOLD EXCESSIVE MEETINGS

Do you love a good meeting?

- One to start the week and one to end it
- One to start the day, and one to end it
- One to share your thoughts, and one for feedback about those thoughts
- One for policy updates, another for information, still another because you want to see the shining faces of your colleagues?

I'll tell you why those faces are shining – they are wet with tears from your excessive meetings.

Do not impose your love of meetings on others. Be a respecter of your colleagues' time.

Rule of thumb: If you hold a meeting, have a specific and clear reason why, an agenda, and an explanation of why those invited need to be present.

Gaining a reputation for holding excessive meetings will negatively impact your reputation as a professional.

How to be *Unprofessional* at work, tip #60:

HOLD **NO** MEETINGS

Imagine a place where you had only one meeting a year with your coworkers. Sound like paradise? Think again.

If you are the boss/manager/CEO/owner, and you despise meetings, too bad.

People on the same team need to meet on a semi-regular basis to be able to have a healthy work environment.

Whether people work remotely, largely independently, or consistently together, there need to be some meetings.

The options aren't constantly meeting or zero meetings. The sweet spot for the number of meetings for your team highly depends on your organization, type of work, and team dynamic.

Talk about it, get curious, and find that golden ratio of meetings (amount, length, subjects to be covered, etc.).

Gaining a reputation for holding no meetings will negatively impact your reputation as a professional.

How to be *Unprofessional* at work, tip #61:

DON'T ASK FOR HELP WHEN YOU NEED IT

Why should you ask for help when you need it? Won't you look:

A. Unprofessional
B. Unprepared
C. Unqualified
D. All of the above?

Answer: E. None of the above

Do you want to know what makes you look incompetent and lacking in self-awareness at work? Not asking for help when you need it.

It is far easier to get clarification/assistance in the beginning than to clean up the mess afterwards.

Whatever it may be, from not knowing how to execute a task to addressing a workplace conflict, the sooner you address it, the better. The sooner you address it, the more you reduce the (potential of greater) harm.

Gaining a reputation for not asking for help when needed will negatively impact your reputation as a professional.

How to be *Unprofessional* at work, tip #62:

What do you get when you lie? Your way... at least for a time.

Once people know you lie, not simply stretching the truth (which is also problematic), but out-and-out lie? That's it.

You will probably be fired. Maybe not for one lie (but maybe). But if you are a habitual liar? Forget about it.

Society and our little microcosm as experienced at work, is built essentially on trust. Without basic trust, you have no ability to move forward as a team or organization.

For example, if you know your company lies to people about paying them for work, then you won't want to work there.

The foundation for all relationships, organizational, communal, governmental, is trust. When you lie, you erode the very foundation you are standing on.

Lying is like peeing in the public pool you're swimming in.

Lying is the coward's way.

Lying is for the weak.

Lying is bad for you and everyone else.

Gaining a reputation for being a liar will TRASH your reputation as a professional.

LEAVE PROJECTS UNFINISH -ED

You got most of it done. The important part at least. What more do people want?

Imagine you were asked to make a peanut butter and jelly sandwich. You get out the ingredients, make the sandwich, deliver it, and then... what? Are you done? Did you put the jelly away? Wipe up the crumbs? Clean off the knife? Making the sandwich is only part of the arc of completing that task.

There are legitimate reasons work projects get abandoned or put on the backburner. But that's not what's at issue here.

The issue here is continually not completing what you are expected to finish at work.

(AKA, Close. The. Loop.)

Gaining a reputation for not finishing projects will negatively impact your reputation as a professional.

DON'T CARE ABOUT THE QUALITY OF YOUR WORK

"D stands for done" is a saying some college students say about classes they have to take but don't care about.

This is an unfortunate attitude and can spill into the "real world" of work. All that matters is that the task is completed. Right?

Wrong. Getting a task completed is only part of the task. It greatly matters how the work gets done, and the quality of your work.

We notice how our colleagues operate. We notice if they do great work, decent work, or barely passable work.

If you don't care about the quality of your work, people will not want to work with you. You will be seen as a liability. Consider that the next time you think no one cares or is watching the way you choose to work.

Gaining a reputation for not caring about the quality of your work will negatively impact your reputation as a professional.

BE
DONE
WITH
LEARNING

You went to school, and now you're out. No more learning for you! Yay!

- Not So Fast -

If you choose to opt out of learning new things in your industry, you will be left behind.

Think about those who choose not to learn new technologies. What do you think about them? What does the marketplace think about them?

They have been left behind, below what is known as The Digital Divide.

Make it a habit NOW to learn and keep up with your field and what's going on in society (hello AI). If you don't, you will become a burden to the others at work and be seen as irrelevant.

Gaining a reputation for not wanting to learn anything new will negatively impact your reputation as a professional.

How to be *Unprofessional* at work, tip #66:

WORK 24/ 7

Work work work work work work work work work work work work work work work work work work work work

Get there first, eat lunch at your desk, leave ... never. Eat, breathe, and barely sleep work. This approach to work is total professionalism, right?

This type of behavior is **NO** badge of honor.

To be your best, most creative and effective self at work, you need separation. If you really work too much, your work and work relationships will suffer.

We know about the detrimental effects of sleep deprivation. We know about the killer impacts of unmanaged stress.

How much work is too much? Well, that depends on a lot.

The point here is that you can work too much. Excessive work can harm your health, home life, and overall work performance. Investigate to discover what is too much (and too little) to find the golden middle ground that works for you.

Gaining a reputation for working 24/7 will negatively impact your reputation as a professional.

How to be *Unprofessional* at work, tip #67:

GO
TO
WORK
SICK

Who would want to go to work sick?

Who thinks this is a good idea?

There are three basic reasons people go to work when they are sick:

1. If I don't work, I don't get paid and can't afford rent, food, etc.
2. If I don't show up to work when sick, my boss will penalize me.
3. If I don't work when I'm sick, the place won't be able to function without me.

This little coffee table book is not really equipped to tackle such large and difficult circumstances people find themselves in, so let me give you a few basic reasons why you should stay home from work when sick.

Basic reason #1: You don't know who you might get sick. It is selfish to not care about those you encounter so much that you don't care if you get them sick.

Basic reason #2: You have an obligation to take care of yourself. With many illnesses, we need rest for our bodies to fight and recover.

Basic reason #3: It's bad for business. If your business encourages/demands sick workers go in to work, people will avoid you like the plague you apparently don't care you're spreading.

Gaining a reputation for going to work sick will negatively impact your reputation as a professional.

DON'T TAKE VACATION

Not taking vacation is a sister to working 24/7.

Taking time-off is human.

Article 24 of the Universal Declaration of Human Rights states "Everyone has the right to rest and leisure, including reasonable limitation of working hours and periodic holidays with pay."

In some cultures, vacation is mandatory.

Why vacation? What is vacation?

Let me ask a different question. What is life for? What are the ingredients of an excellent human life?

Taking time off for rest, relaxation, and taking part in the activities of your culture are important parts of the pieces that make up an excellent life.

Taking vacation will actually help you be better at work. (And, if your organization makes you feel bad for taking vacation or "punishes" you for taking vacation, they are in the wrong and broken. Shame on them.)

Gaining a reputation for not taking vacation will negatively impact your reputation as a professional.

How to be *Unprofessional* at work, tip #69:

ASSUME WORK CANNOT FUNCTION WITHOUT YOU

This place will FALL APART WITHOUT ME.

I am completely irreplaceable. I'm the one doing all the work. I'm the one that is holding this place together.

You are the only you. YOU ARE AMAZING. Your organization has the feel that it has because of you.

But assuming your business **needs** you sets both you and your organization up for failure. Professionals empower those around them and make the place better, not co-dependent on them.

Many people with this mentality have a rude awakening when they get laid off... or fired.

The fact of the matter is, AT WORK, you are replaceable. The organization can fire you in a heartbeat or the business may fail, and you'll be out of a job.

Thinking yourself irreplaceable makes taking vacation, personal, and sick days hard to impossible.

Work to find that balance of being an asset, wherever you work. Resist the urge to make the place you work 100% dependent on you.

Gaining a reputation for acting as if the organization can't function without you will negatively impact your reputation as a professional.

GATEKEEP DATA

Hoarding information.

This is a time and tested strategy for feeling important at work and trying to shore up job security.

In the short run, keeping the information to yourself may seem like you are cleverly and firmly entrenching your place in the organization, making you indispensable.

But in the long run, when you don't share information, people can't do their job effectively.

Gatekeeping information also causes needless frustration, unnecessary uncertainty, and pointless quarrels. Excellent workers leave, creativity is reduced, people wander away from executing the company mission effectively... shall I continue?

Don't hoard information.

Share information unless you have a genuinely good reason not to.

Gaining a reputation for gatekeeping information will negatively impact your reputation as a professional.

DON'T
BE
TRANSPARENT

Isn't it good to keep people guessing?

Isn't it exciting to not really know where people stand, what their motives are, why the organization is doing what they're doing?

No. You are not in a British murder mystery story. You are not a child. You're a grown adult at work.

In order for everyone to do their job excellently, they need to clearly know what's going on and why.

MANAGERS, let your workers know what's going on and why.

WORKERS, let your managers know what's going on and why.

MEMBERS OF THE BOARD, let everyone know what's going on and why.

Being transparent and not hoarding information are cousins. Just as you should give people as much information as possible (in the right way at the right time), let people know **WHY** you're doing what you're doing. No hiding. No lying. Be up front.

Gaining a reputation for not being transparent will negatively impact your reputation as a professional.

BE
UNAPPROAH
-ABLE

To have power at work, shouldn't people be just a little bit afraid of you?

I mean, just imagine if everyone thought they could swing by, at any time, and chat, chat, chat. How could you get any work done?

This is a legitimate worry. But let's make a distinction between being unapproachable and being a pushover. There's certainly a happy medium between these two extremes, and this is what you want at work.

If you are unsociable and aloof at work, you're likely to be branded some kind of diva. Divas don't have the best reputation for being team players.

This book you're reading is set in the here and now. This is not a playbook from yesteryear. The future, the real future of work and having a long career, is in finding a way to work with others.

If people are afraid to approach you, something is wrong. I have no idea what that is. I've never met you. But you are just a person, and you are no better than anybody else. There is no reason people need to feel fear in a work environment just to ask you questions or interact with you.

Cultivating a persona of fear swirling around you is immature. Move into the future.

Gaining a reputation for being unapproachable will negatively impact your reputation as a professional.

How to be *Unprofessional* at work, tip #73:

ASSUME NEGATIVE INTENT FROM OTHERS

You're late because you have a good reason, right? Maybe you couldn't find your keys, or your kid couldn't find a shoe, or the power went out in the middle of getting ready for work, etc.

But that colleague you already don't like, why are they late? Well, that's just how they are. They don't care about anyone but themselves. We all know they have a poor work ethic, and showing up late, yet again, is just more proof they are awful (as if you needed more proof).

We tend to grant our mistakes grace and understanding because we know we have good intentions, while with the mistakes of others we tend to assume they have negative intentions.

Stop it.

Stop thinking you're a mind reader. You aren't. You don't know why someone is acting in a particular way.

Assigning negative intentions to someone at work will only serve to get in your way of solving issues and moving forward at work.

Gaining a reputation for assigning negative intentions to coworkers' actions will negatively impact your reputation as a professional.

How to be *Unprofessional* at work, tip #74:

ROLL
YOUR
EYES

"Come on, Merry," you say. "You can't be serious! If you only knew who I worked with, your eyes would be rolling out of your head!"

Yes, we all experience coworkers we find *challenging*. In most places you'll have colleagues that irritate you, annoy you, and whom you find burdensome.

Work is not a fairytale land where you get to remake your coworkers in your image.

Heck – you don't even have to really like your coworkers to have a fruitful and heathy work environment.

So, what do you do about those coworkers who drive you crazy????

The answer lies with you. This is essentially a **YOU** problem.

You are responsible for how you interact with others. **You** are responsible for your reactions and emotional responses. **You**, as an adult, need to treat everyone with dignity and baseline respect.

A sure sign of immaturity is rolling your eyes at a colleague behind their back (or to their face). My advice to all of the eye rollers: realize this is your immaturity leaking out and address it.

Gaining a reputation for rolling your eyes at colleagues will negatively impact your reputation as a professional.

How to be *Unprofessional* at work, tip #75:

BE
STINKY

What it means to "smell appropriate" at work depends on where you work, the kind of work, and the cultural norms around you.

There are many reasons why someone may be "stinky" at work such as:
- Health issues
- Lack of access to laundry facilities
- Cultural differences
- Differences about what does/doesn't smell good

Stinkiness is highly individual. A perfume might smell like heaven to one coworker while giving another a migraine.

Addressing how someone smells is very tricky, but we do no favors to the individual if their odor is causing problems and we remain silent.

Given this HIGHLY SENSITIVE topic, **MUCH** care, thought and planning need to occur before you address this issue. But address it. The sooner the better.

Is your odor getting in the way with clients, colleagues, and promotions? If you aren't sure, ask someone who will tell you the truth. Warning: most people won't tell you the truth about this.

Gaining a reputation for being "stinky" will negatively impact your reputation as a professional.

DON'T WELCOME QUESTIONS

Why should you want people to question you? If people question you, it's a sign of disrespect, right? Like they're trying to micromanage you, right? If they trusted you, there would be no questions.

Wrong.

Genuine curiosity is good. Questions that aren't passive-aggressive are good.

If you are a leader, set the tone and expectation for your team that you see questions as a sign of caring and engagement **instead of a threat**.

If you are part of a team, let others know by the way you act that you are interested in answering questions. Welcoming questions nondefensively is a way to demonstrate you care about the work and your team members.

Questions are only a threat if you turn them into threats. If people think you are unapproachable, everyone suffers.

Gaining a reputation for not being open to questions will negatively impact your reputation as a professional.

How to be *Unprofessional* at work, tip #77:

RIDICULE OTHERS

- Mocking colleagues
- Laughing at them
- Pointing out their flaws publicly
- Humiliating coworkers
- Insulting them

Such workplace behavior is a fast track to being left behind in your career.

It may feel good, and others may laugh with you as you feel you are King of the Office, but this is temporary.

When you degrade colleagues through your speech, you deflate them and erode their will to support you. People become disengaged and wither. They will not give you their best effort or work, not really. And any chance they get, they will turn on you. (For a good example of this, read Machiavelli's *The Prince*).

If you are not sure whether your "jokes" are landing and might be considered hostile, ask someone who will tell you the truth. Warning: many people feel uncomfortable telling others hard truths.

Gaining a reputation for ridiculing colleagues will negatively impact your reputation as a professional.

How to be *Unprofessional* at work, tip #78:

EXPECT ALL TO THINK LIKE YOU

You are a rational person.
Rational people have rational beliefs.
Therefore, my beliefs are rational.
Therefore, if people don't see the world the way I see it, they are irrational.

Incorrect.

Unfortunately, we tend to fall into this trap of thinking everyone should view the world the way that we do. Everyone should think like we think because we're reasonable and they should recognize this truth and fall in line.

Well, you do have good thoughts. And so does your neighbor. Yet not everybody agrees with you at work, and it's not because they're irrational fools. It's because we have different experiences, different values, different perspectives, ETC.

The professional not only lives and let lives, they welcome a diversity of ideas. Even when those ideas conflict with their own.

Gaining a reputation for expecting everyone to think just like you will negatively impact your reputation as a professional.

How to be *Unprofessional* at work, tip #79:

COMPLAIN

It's too hot.
It's too cold.
It's too hard.
It's too boring.
It's not fair.
I don't want to do it.
That's not my job.

Sure. We have legitimate complaints that need to be addressed. Sometimes a work environment **is** too hot, not fair, too hard, too demanding, etc. In those instances, **we should speak up.**

A problem arises when we are constantly complaining and never have any solutions.

Here are two rules of thumb to consider before you complain to your boss:

Rule of thumb #1: Think carefully and thoughtfully before you complain.

Rule of thumb #2: Come up with possible and workable solutions before you speak with your boss.

Gaining a reputation for being an excessive complainer will negatively impact your reputation as a professional.

How to be *Unprofessional* at work, tip #80:

SET IMPOSSIBLY HIGH STANDARDS

All I demand is constant vigilance and excellence. What's wrong with that? Isn't that the very definition and essence of a professional?

And besides, I don't hold others to a standard I don't hold myself to.

High standards – YES

Impossibly high standards – NO

If your standards are too high and people are expected to be perfect, then you are acting as if you are not working with human persons.

But you are. All people make mistakes.

If there is no way to acknowledge and make room for mistakes, guess what happens? MORE MISTAKES!

If your standards are *too high*, people won't admit when something is wrong, which disincentivizes taking responsibility for actions and fixing the problem so it doesn't happen in the future.

If your standards are impossible to realize, many people won't even try because they are doomed to fail before they begin.

Yes – you can have standards that are too high. Instead, set excellent, yet reasonable, standards.

Gaining a reputation for setting impossibly high standards will negatively impact your reputation as a professional.

HOW
TO
BE
PROFESSIONAL
AT
WORK

How to be **PROFESSONAL** at work:

ASK FOR HELP

I don't want to leave you without **my #1 tip** for being a professional at work: **ask for help**.

- Ask for help when you don't know what to do.
- Ask for help when you experience physical problems.
- Ask for help when you have mental health concerns.

You do not need to suffer in silence. If anyone tells you differently, get away from them.

ALL of us need help from time to time. We may need help repairing a leaky roof, fixing a car, preparing a tax return, learning to play an instrument, addressing mental and physical health concerns, and the list goes on and on.

You are more than where you work.

You are more than your job.

Whatever kind of help you may need, reach out. If someone says "no," move to the next person.

You are worth it.
You have infinite value and worth.
Seek help until you find it.

Peace to you.

Closing Thoughts

<u>What do you think?</u>
Is it too hard to be a professional? I've listed 80 ways to make mistakes, and I'm already writing a companion to this book, containing more behaviors to avoid. The list of what to steer clear of can feel endless.

<u>So... is it worth it to be a professional?</u>
Yes! The real advantage in being a professional is in a life well lived. When we treat ourselves, those around us, and our community with respect and care, everyone wins.

<u>What if you don't care about the job you're in?</u>
Not every job is our "dream" job. However, I suggest caring about yourself, your future, and treating others well. You may be surprised how much you learn and the beneficial connections you make when you act professionally at work.

<u>What if you don't want to be a so-called professional?</u>
Sometimes we think acting "professionally" is only for people in suits in large, high-rise buildings. I disagree. Being a professional is about how people conduct themselves at work – any work. There are plenty of "so-called professionals" in ties who act unprofessionally, and tons of people in service industries who are absolute pros! Don't be fooled by job titles.

You are a professional only if you act like one. What choice do you make?

AI and Me

In early 2023, I was thinking about what it means to be a professional at work, and the surrounding confusion. As a (recovering?) philosopher, when I don't know what something is, I think of what something is not to start the process of eliminating wrong answers on my journey to find the right ones. I came up with an initial list of what counts as unprofessional behavior.

Right around this time, I first started using ChatGPT. I asked it for more examples of unprofessional behavior. I added those suggestions into my initial list, and other suggestions made by the LLM. The result is this book. "How to Be Unprofessional at Work: Tips to Ensure Failure" contains mostly my work, but in collaboration with ChatGPT.

Acknowledgements

After teaching philosophy for over 20 years, in 2021 I left the profession at the end of the spring semester and pursued my new vocation: workplace conflict resolution work.

Over the past two years, I have come to appreciate the incredible power of networking and the profound joy of building connections.

I want to express my heartfelt gratitude to the remarkable individuals who have played a significant role in this transformative journey. Mandy Hinson, Landy Fuqua, Scott Williams, Gemma Bromfield, David Liddle, Lindsay Frillings, Marsh Naidoo, Brooke Simmons, Sandy Tarkington, Jonathan Rodrigues, Courtney Echols, Suzanne Harper, and the professionals who generously shared their time and expertise on my podcast, Conflict Managed, have my deepest thanks.

Thank you to my readers for gifting me your time, care, and expertise: Lisa Smartt, Jeremiah Whiteman, Alesia McDonough, Patricia Brown, Stephanie Richardson, and Christopher M. Brown.

To all those mentioned here, my family, and the countless others who have impacted my journey, your belief, guidance, and friendship have been invaluable. I am immensely grateful for the connections we have formed and the experiences we have shared.

About the Author

Merry Brown is a writer, speaker, mediator, founder and owner of **Third Party Workplace Conflict Restoration Services**, and host of **Conflict Managed**, a weekly podcast about toxic work environments and how to fix them.
In addition to "How to Be Unprofessional at Work: Tips to Ensure Failure" she is the author of "The Food Addict: Recovering from Binge Eating Disorder & Making Peace with Food" as well as two young adult series, featuring "The Knowers" and "Gold Manor Ghost House."

She has a B.A. from Azusa Pacific University in Philosophy and Psychology and an M.A. in Humanities with an emphasis in Philosophy from Western Kentucky University.

Connect with Merry Brown
Email: 3pconflictrestoration@gmail.com
Website: 3pconflictrestoration.com
LinkedIn: linkedin.com/in/merry-brown
TikTok: @3pconflictrestoriation
Conflict Managed Podcast is available wherever you listen to podcasts

Made in the USA
Monee, IL
14 October 2024

67917138R00104